WHAT THE BIBLE SAYS ABOUT

Marriage Divorce & Remarriage

D1622506

John Coblentz

Cover Artist
Ruth Yoder

Christian Light Publications, Inc.
Harrisonburg, VA 22801

ISBN: 0-87813-544-8
Printed in USA

CONTENTS

i

CONTENTS, continued

CHRISTIAN FAMILY LIVING SERIES

Christian Family Living

This basic book of the series offers practical Scriptural help ranging from training toddlers to caring for aging parents. Each chapter closes with questions for further thought and action.

God's Will for My Body—Guidance for Adolescents

A workbook to help parents in teaching their children about adolescent changes.

God's Will for Love in Marriage—Cultivating Marital Intimacy

A study guide for engaged persons or married couples, offering practical, Biblical guidance for healthy intimacy in marriage. Includes a frank, Biblical approach to the controversial subject of family planning.

Courtship That Glorifies God—A Biblical Approach to Dating and Engagement

A reprint of Chapter 3 in *Christian Family Living*. Available as a booklet for study in youth groups, Bible schools, high schools, etc.

Singlehood That Glorifies God—Living With Eternal Purpose

A reprint of Chapter 4 in *Christian Family*

Living. This booklet is for single people as well as for those willing to understand and respect single people.

What the Bible Says About Marriage, Divorce, and Remarriage

A Biblical approach to a battered subject, this study follows a question-and-answer format in showing what the Bible says and in offering practical help for resolving difficult situations.

INTRODUCTION

Imagine the joy the Creator must have had in making the first man and woman and teaching them about marriage, commitment, and families. Consider, then, what sorrow He must have had as men and women began perverting themselves and violating their marriage commitments. Contemplate the Creator of men and women as He observes the current situation in the Western world—unfaithful partners . . . broken marriages . . . hurting, scared, scarred, embittered children . . . the live-in, shack-up, come-and-go mentality.

This Creator God has not been silent on these issues. In His Word He has clearly laid out the guidelines by which marriage, home, and family are to operate.

In an attempt to cope with the distresses which sin, self, and immorality have thrown us into, man has offered a variety of solutions to marriage problems—trial marriages, no-fault divorce, counseling centers, family services, support groups, etc. But with rare exception, these "solutions" ignore God's laws and principles regarding marriage and instead attempt to make the wayward ways of man work better. This is like trying to treat a bad appendix with pain reliever. Man's solutions are not treating root problems, but instead in many cases are actually contributing to them.

The church is not free from people with marriage problems. Whatever the cause—whether the problems come because church members are living too close to the world or because people with a heritage of the world are coming to Jesus—the reality remains: the church today must know what it believes about marriage, divorce, and remarriage. We are faced increasingly with people having marriage problems and entanglements.

The church, unfortunately, has not been united in its message to those in troubled marriages. Some religious people have adopted the world's solutions. Others have tried to take a common-sense approach. And still others have tried to stand with one leg on God's Word and the other on human solutions. What IS the proper approach? Where are the answers to these problems?

This writing proceeds on several basic premises:

1. That God's Word provides the laws and principles by which marriage, home, and family are to operate. "For he established a testimony in Jacob, and appointed a law in Israel, which he commanded our fathers, that they should make them known to their children: That the generation to come might know them, even the children which should be born; who should arise and declare them to their children" (Psalm 78:5, 6).

2. That God's Word is always right, and we do not have the option of altering it. "Therefore I esteem all thy precepts concerning all things to be right" (Psalm 119:128).

3. That marriages and families will be blessed or

troubled according to how they honor God's principles. "The generation of the upright shall be blessed" (Psalm 112:2). "He that turneth away his ear from hearing the law, even his prayer shall be abomination" (Proverbs 28:9).

4. That persisting in sin brings serious consequences. "Know ye not that the unrighteous shall not inherit the kingdom of God? Be not deceived: neither fornicators, nor idolaters, nor adulterers, nor effeminate, nor abusers of themselves with mankind . . ." (I Corinthians 6:9).

5. That those who repent of their sin will find God's forgiveness. "And such were some of you: but ye are washed, but ye are sanctified, but ye are justified in the name of the Lord Jesus, and by the Spirit of our God" (I Corinthians 6:11).

In light of all of the above premises, we must look honestly and humbly at the Word of God to find answers to the problems we encounter in marriages and homes today.

MARRIAGE

WHAT IS MARRIAGE?

1. Marriage is the joining of an unmarried man with an unmarried woman to form a home of their own.

"Therefore shall a man leave his father and his mother, and shall cleave unto his wife: and they shall be one flesh" (Genesis 2:24). "Thou shalt go unto my country, and to my kindred, and take a wife unto my son Isaac . . . . And they called Rebekah, and said unto her, Wilt thou go with this man? And she said, I will go. . . . And Isaac brought her into his mother Sarah's tent, and took Rebekah, and she became his wife; and he loved her" (Genesis 24:4, 58, 67). Whatever else we may conclude from these Scriptures, we can safely say that marriage is the joining of a man and woman in a lifelong bond. The man and woman leave the home of their father and mother and establish a home of their own.

2. Marriage is a covenant relationship for life.

"Set me as a seal upon thine heart, as a seal upon thine arm: for love is strong as death; jealousy is cruel as the grave" (Song of Solomon 8:6).

"Yet is she thy companion, and the wife of thy covenant" (Malachi 2:14).

"For the woman which hath an husband is bound by the law to her husband so long as he liveth; but if the husband be dead, she is loosed from the law of her husband" (Romans 7:2).

Marriage is not only the joining of a man and woman, but it is also a covenant to be faithful in that union for life. There is a proper jealousy in marital love, an exclusiveness which says in effect, "The love which I give to you I will give to no other, and the love which you give to me, you must give to no other."

We might note here that while this exclusiveness is prescribed in the Bible, it is also to a certain extent inherent in marital love. There is an unwritten but very evident expectation of faithfulness in the love between a man and a woman. It is ironic that this generation which so sings the praises of love with no strings attached is also saturated with songs of heartache, betrayal, and disappointment and regularly hears the news of violence and murder due to the unfaithfulness of these "lovers."

In light of the covenantal requirement in marriage, such variations as trial marriages or contract

2

marriages, which place limitations on time or responsibilities, violate what the Bible teaches about marriage. These contracts form a cooperative relationship, but fall short of the lifetime oneness and commitment required in marriage. From a Biblical standpoint, therefore, a contract marriage would not be a true marriage, but rather, an illicit relationship.

3. Marriage begins with an event (a wedding) which marks for the couple and for observers a change from singlehood to marriage.

"And the third day there was a marriage in Cana of Galilee; and the mother of Jesus was there: And both Jesus was called, and his disciples, to the marriage" (John 2:1, 2).

We have seen that marriage is the joining of a man and woman and that it includes a lifelong commitment. Now we are noting what at first thought may seem obvious: marriage has a particular ceremony, announcement, feast, or suchlike event which marks its beginning. This event may vary in its details from culture to culture, but for both the couple and the public, it marks the beginning of the marriage. Before it, the two are recognized as single and unmarried, but afterward, they are known to be joined in marriage.

In the Bible, any relationship which assumes privileges of marriage before the wedding is considered a morally wrong relationship. It is not considered valid marriage. Thus, a "common-law marriage" is not true marriage. Even when recognized by the state as official (after a given time of cohabitation), it fails to meet Biblical criteria. The line between fornication and marriage is virtually impossible to draw if the beginning of marriage is not marked by a particular event, by some form of a wedding.

4. Marriage should include those social or civil steps which make it a legitimate marriage in one's society.

In the Book of Ruth we find Boaz taking careful socio-civil steps in his marriage to Ruth (see Ruth 3:12, 13; 4:1-11). Jewish social practices by the time of Christ included a covenant with witnesses at the time of espousal and a feast with family and friends at the time of marriage. Although the Bible does not prescribe any socio-civil steps for marriage, we can assume God's people have followed and should follow social propriety and civil guidelines in getting married. (See also Romans 13:1.)

As we noted in the preceding point, civil law may recognize as valid that which does not meet Biblical requirements (as in a common-law marriage), but a valid marriage should include those social and civil steps which make the marriage legitimate in society.

In North America, this would include public announcements (usually following an espousal), a marriage license, a ceremony performed by a recognized minister or magistrate, and an official record of the ceremony.

5. Marriage gives the right to experience the bond of physical union.

"Therefore shall a man leave his father and his mother, and shall cleave unto his wife: and they shall be one flesh" (Genesis 2:24).

"Let the husband render unto the wife due benevolence: and likewise also the wife unto the husband. The wife hath not power of her own body, but the husband: and likewise also the husband hath not power of his own body, but the wife. Defraud ye not one the other" (I Corinthians 7:3-5).

On the basis of the above Scriptures, some people consider physical union integral to marriage, so that if no sexual relations follow the wedding ceremony, it is not a valid marriage.

The point is debatable. Rather than absolutely requiring physical union for marriage, the Bible would rather seem to expect it. The sexual relationship is a very fundamental and tangible expression of the oneness and commitment of marriage, and to deprive one another sexually in marriage is wrong.

Others have carried the point of physical union even further, saying that it IS the marriage bond, that those who have a sexual relationship have formed a marriage bond. According to I Corinthians 6:16, sexual relations certainly do form a bond (for which cause harlotry is not merely a sinful act, but a sinful bond), but the Bible does not equate marriage with sexual union. This is clear in Exodus 22:16, 17, where it says if a man has sexual relations with a virgin, he has the obligation to take her to be his wife unless her father refuses. Then he must pay the price of her dowry. The point is clear: by doing to her what only a husband ought to do, he owes her all the obligations of a husband, but his sin does not automatically make him her husband.

WHAT ARE BIBLICAL PURPOSES FOR MARRIAGE?

1. God arranged marriage for procreation.

"Male and female created he them. And God blessed them, and God said unto them, Be fruitful, and multiply, and replenish the earth" (Genesis 1:27, 28).

"Thy wife shall be as a fruitful vine by the sides of thine house: thy children like olive plants round about thy table. Behold, that thus shall the man be blessed that feareth the LORD" (Psalm 128:3, 4).

God arranged marriage to propagate the human

race. The attempts to "safeguard" modern marriages from the experiences of childbearing and child rearing (or severely limiting family size) in the interests of maintaining Western life-style have directly and indirectly made many marriages hollow. The pro-sex/anti-children attitude has contributed much to the disintegration of marriage and family life.

2. God ordained marriage to meet some of our most basic human needs.

"Let every one of you in particular so love his wife even as himself; and the wife see that she reverence her husband" (Ephesians 5:33).

"And, ye fathers, provoke not your children to wrath: but bring them up in the nurture and admonition of the Lord" (Ephesians 6:4).

"She looketh well to the ways of her household, and eateth not the bread of idleness. Her children arise up, and call her blessed; her husband also, and he praiseth her" (Proverbs 31:27, 28).

God's purposes for children as the fruit of marriage extend beyond the mere fact of populating the world. People need other people. As marriage takes place in love and commitment according to God's design, homes are established, children are born, and the family becomes the center of social interaction, old and young mingling and relating in the variety of life's activities.

Humans have daily needs for food, clothing, shelter, and rest. On a deeper level, we need love, acceptance, a sense of belonging, encouragement, understanding, and security. God ordained marriage and the home to be a center where these needs are met. Parents provide for their children food, clothes, love, security, etc., and the children provide for their parents opportunities and responsibilities for which manhood and womanhood were made. Husband and wife provide intimate acceptance and love needs in the bonds of marriage. Thus, marriage, home, and family become the setting for growth and maturity from infancy to old age, generation after generation.

3. God planned marriage to establish a stable center of learning from generation to generation.

"And these words, which I command thee this day, shall be in thine heart: And thou shalt teach them diligently unto thy children, and shalt talk of them when thou sittest in thine house, and when thou walkest by the way, and when thou liest down, and when thou risest up" (Deuteronomy 6:6, 7).

"We will not hide them from their children, shewing to the generation to come the

8

praises of the LORD, and his strength, and his wonderful works that he hath done. For he established a testimony in Jacob, and appointed a law in Israel, which he commanded our fathers, that they should make them known to their children: That the generation to come might know them, even the children which should be born; who should arise and declare them to their children: That they might set their hope in God, and not forget the works of God, but keep his commandments" (Psalm 78:4-7).

Children are learners. They need teachers who instruct them in ways of truth and righteousness. God planned that the husband and wife as a teaching / training team raise their children in His ways for His glory. It takes failure in only one generation for the knowledge of God to be cut off from succeeding generations.

4. God planned marriage to be a picture of the relationship of Christ and the church.

"Wives, submit yourselves unto your own husbands, as unto the Lord. For the husband is the head of the wife, even as Christ is the head of the church: and he is the saviour of the body. Therefore as the church is subject unto Christ, so let the wives be to their own husbands in every thing. Husbands, love

9

your wives, even as Christ also loved the church, and gave himself for it. . . . This is a great mystery: but I speak concerning Christ and the church" (Ephesians 5:22-25, 32).

God often uses the tangible to illustrate the spiritual. He commanded Moses, for example, to make the tabernacle exactly according to plan in order to faithfully typify the realities of the New Covenant. Even so marriage today must follow God's directions faithfully to typify the spiritual reality of Christ's relationship to the church. This analogy often provides practical guidance in working through problems in marriage.

HOW IS MARRIAGE BEING UNDERMINED IN WESTERN CULTURE TODAY?

The home is a basic unit of society. It follows then that the deterioration of homes results in the deterioration of society and that general deterioration in society likewise undermines homes. The Apostle Paul warned numerous times in his writings about the peril of social deterioration in the last days. While most of these warnings are about society in general, they all affect the home as a unit of society, and some of them speak to family relations in particular.

"This know also, that in the last days perilous times shall come. For men shall be lovers of their own selves, covetous, boasters, proud, blasphemers, disobedient to parents, unthankful, unholy, without natural affection, trucebreakers, false accusers, incontinent, fierce, despisers of those that are good, traitors, heady, highminded, lovers of pleasures more than lovers of God; having a form of godliness, but denying the power thereof: from such turn away" (II Timothy 3:1-5).

1. Marriage is being undermined today because people are lovers of their own selves.

Modern psychology has assured us that self needs are primary needs. We are told we need self-esteem, a good self-image, self-confidence, self-actualization, and self-love. All-important is the need to accomplish MY goals, to realize MY full potential. This focus on self is exactly what the natural man does not need. It lies at the heart of much of the discontent, irritation, and frustration in the modern home. The world fortunately doesn't revolve around any one human being.

Christ calls us to deny ourselves to follow Him. That doesn't make for very popular psychology, but it is basic to Christianity. There is a grain of truth in the self-talk. We do have inner yearnings for acceptance and fulfillment. But according to the Scriptures, we find those needs met, not by serving ourselves, but by serving God and others.

We need the mind of Jesus, "Who, being in the form of God . . . made himself of no reputation, and took upon him the form of a servant, and was made in the likeness of men" (Philippians 2:6, 7).

2. Marriage is being undermined today because people are covetous.

Covetousness is the opposite of contentment. Discontent is fostered in children with multiplied toys and pleasures and in adolescents with bigger toys and spicier pleasures. It is hardly a wonder, then, that adults grow discontented with one life-long companion. How can we expect married people not to covet someone else's companion if they have spent their whole life in patterns of discontent and covetousness?

In our day people not only want things they do not have, but they demand things they do not have. The mood is one of instant gratification. People seldom see the tie between covetousness and hostility, but invariably when material things and personal wants have priority, relationships suffer.

3. Marriage is being undermined today because people are disobedient to parents.

This speaks directly to children and may be applied to anything from the tantrums of two-year-olds to the rebellion of sixteen-year-olds. We must not understand this, however, to mean that somehow a batch of bad babies will be born in the last days. Children have always been children. But in the last days, their disobedience will not be restrained. The problem is a pattern of disrespect for parents, regardless of age.

Children are in many ways a reflection of their parents. Disregard for parents, disrespect, and disobedience are not the exclusive problems of those under twenty-one. The disobedient children are only mirroring the disrespect and general disobedience of the age. In any case, the disobedient mindset wrecks the respect, order, and peace which should grace the home.

4. Marriage is being undermined today because people are without natural affection.

The literal understanding of "without natural affection" is "without natural human affection." It refers specifically to paternal love and the natural ties between close kin. We are seeing this prophecy unfold today in the heart-wrenching accounts of battered wives and abused children. We are seeing it, furthermore, in the abortion clinics, where in the United States alone, 171 rejected babies each hour around the clock are being snipped apart by the abortionist's shears, drowned in saline solution, or torn limb from limb.

God has given humans a natural affection for their kin, which calls for strong family loyalty and loving parent-child bonds. In a self-seeking age, these natural affections are choked out by the love of money, love of career, love of pleasure, love of going, love of getting, love of the world. Instead of strong family love, therefore, we have those families who split apart as by whim, those parents who can tolerate only one or two children and who gladly farm out their children to baby-sitters and day-care centers while they pursue their own interests — void of natural affection.

5. Marriage is being undermined today because people are truce breakers.

Commitment in relationships gets a poor following today. Self, sex, and sin are more important to many people than honesty, faithfulness, and integrity. "I promise" means "that's how I feel today, but tomorrow I may feel different." It is on the shoals of broken promises and shattered commitments that homes and marriages are wrecked.

Notice that the list in II Timothy 3 also includes "traitors." A traitor is one who gives the appearance of loyalty, but in reality is working for personal interests. Trucebreakers and traitors use bargaining, lies, betrayal, flattery, bribes, bluffs, and such tactics to accomplish their ends. Homes today are rife with broken hearts and scarred lives as a result of truce breakers and traitors.

6. Marriage is being undermined today because people are lovers of pleasures more than lovers of God.

No one in America today would deny that people are pleasure-minded. Fun mania has swept the land. It feeds the self-seeking, give-me attitudes and so doing undermines the love, commitment, and sacrifice necessary for strong marriages. The strong doses of entertainment our culture gulps down are detrimental, however, not only because they feed selfishness and erode godliness, but often because of the vulgarity of the entertainment itself.

Movies, television, radio programs, videos, novels, and love songs of our day regularly and unceasingly show flirting, betrayal, unfaithfulness, extramarital sex, divorce, and even sexual perversions as entertainment. Such entertainment directly undermines marriage and homes. Children and adults who regularly live in an immoral imaginative world sooner or later find these things becoming a part of real life for them.

Unfortunately, many "Christians" are blind to the effects of pleasure-mindedness. In their blindness, they do not see any contradiction between their profession of life in Christ and their love of worldly pleasures. The Apostle Paul's warning concerning such people is pointed. "She that liveth in pleasure is dead while she liveth" (I Timothy 5:6).

7. Marriage is being undermined today by those who have "vile affections."

The Apostle Paul also wrote to the Romans about those with "vile affections." We do well to ponder the relationship between the increase of homosexuality in modern society and the breakdown of the home. The passage in Romans states:

"God gave them up unto vile affections: for even their women did change the natural use into that which is against nature: And likewise also the men, leaving the natural use of the woman, burned in their lust one toward another; men with men working that which is unseemly" (Romans 1:26, 27).

We might ask why there is an increase in homosexuality today. The preoccupation with sex and self in our culture inadvertently empties relationships of meaning and commitment. In the absence of meaningful commitment, marriage for many people is unfulfilling and even pointless. Sex is the thing, and where sex is given this kind of priority, natural affections easily move to the unnatural. Inordinate sex drives, whether in heterosexual relationships or homosexual, are ruinous to marriage. Love gives way to lust, and when lusts are followed, people inevitably get hurt.

The influence of "vile affections" on our culture, however, cannot be measured simply by the number of homosexuals there are. Unisex trends are seen in simple things such as clothing styles and hairstyles, as well as in the more complex matter of male and female roles. Vile affection, in other words, is having its impact on society as a whole, not merely on a few perverted individuals

To state these points positively, we could say that if marriages and homes are to be stable and strong, they must:
—Focus on serving God and others as a means of fulfillment.
—Practice contentedness with regard to material things.
— Respect the authority of parents, including the counsel of grandparents.
—Nurture healthy, loving ties between all family members.
—Value faithfulness and fidelity in marriage commitments.
—Love God supremely and refuse worldly pleasures—"the lust of the flesh, and the lust of the eyes, and the pride of life" (I John 2:16).
—Honor God's moral standards, accepting the Biblical pattern for the roles of men and women and refusing all forms of sexual perversion.

DIVORCE

DOES THE BIBLE EVER PERMIT DIVORCE?

God made the man and the woman specifically to complement each other in marriage. Concerning divorce, Jesus said unequivocally, "From the beginning it was not so" (Matthew 19:8). God did not say to Adam, "Now I made this woman to be your wife, but if your marriage doesn't work out, you may divorce her, and we'll try another rib!"

The Scriptural account of God making a suitable companion for Adam concludes with the statement, "Therefore shall a man leave his father and his mother, and shall cleave unto his wife: and they shall be one flesh" (Genesis 2:24). This speaks clearly of lifelong fidelity.

The first instructions regarding divorce came under the leadership of Moses.

"When a man hath taken a wife, and married her, and it come to pass that she find no favour in his eyes, because he hath found some uncleanness in her: then let him write her a bill of divorcement, and give it in her

18

hand, and send her out of his house. And when she is departed out of his house, she may go and be another man's wife. And if the latter husband hate her, and write her a bill of divorcement, and giveth it in her hand, and sendeth her out of his house; or if the latter husband die, which took her to be his wife; her former husband, which sent her away, may not take her again to be his wife, after that she is defiled; for that is abomination before the LORD: and thou shalt not cause the land to sin, which the LORD thy God giveth thee for an inheritance" (Deuteronomy 24:1-4).

This Scripture taken by itself might be understood as giving sanction to divorce—that it is all right. We will note shortly, however, that God says He hates divorce. When we look at the above Scripture with this in view, we can acknowledge that it does not say divorce is all right. It prescribes some regulations for divorce:

1. Divorce could be only by official action, requiring a written document.
2. Divorce granted the right to remarry.
3. After remarriage, the divorcee could never return to the former partner.

In cultures around Israel at this time, women sometimes were considered little more than property to be bartered or traded or retained according to the pleasure of men. In Hebrew culture, however, a man was not free to send away his wife and bring her back at his whim. The "bill of divorcement" gave her legal protection from such abuses.

WHAT DOES GOD THINK OF DIVORCE?

"The LORD hath been witness between thee and the wife of thy youth, against whom thou hast dealt treacherously: yet is she thy companion, and the wife of thy covenant. And did not he make one? Yet had he the residue of the spirit. And wherefore one? That he might seek a godly seed. Therefore take heed to your spirit, and let none deal treacherously against the wife of his youth. For the LORD, the God of Israel, saith that he hateth putting away" (Malachi 2:14-16).

In Malachi, God is rebuking the Israelites for their unfaithfulness to Him. As a people, they had joined themselves to strange gods. This was spiritual adultery. Their unfaithful spirit showed in their marriages also. As they put away God, so they were putting away their wives. Isn't that a logical consequence? Covenant breakers on one level of relationship will break covenant on other levels of relationship. Therefore, GOD HATES PUTTING AWAY. Divorce spells unfaithfulness, treachery, betrayal, and love grown cold. God wants people who are faithful, true, and constant in their love. In many ways the spiritual stature of people can be measured by the way they act in their marriage.

God's attitude toward divorce is demonstrated also in that, although He permitted divorce under Moses, He forbade it for the priests. "They shall not take a wife that is a whore, or profane; neither shall they take a woman put away from her husband: for he is holy unto his God" (Leviticus 21:7). Divorce is clearly recognized here as unholy—that which would make a priest ineligible for service in the house of God. Again, God hates divorce.

IF GOD HATES DIVORCE, WHY DID HE PERMIT IT?

"And the Pharisees came to him, and asked him, Is it lawful for a man to put away his wife? tempting him. And he answered and said unto them, What did Moses command you? And they said, Moses suffered to write a bill of divorcement, and to put her away. And Jesus answered and said unto them, For the hardness of your heart he wrote you this precept" (Mark 10:2-5).

Here we have the resolution to the problem of divorce being permitted under Moses although it was despised by God. Divorce was never sanctioned, but under the Old Covenant God permitted it because of the hard hearts of the people of

Israel. God permitted it in anticipation of the New Testament era in which He would require a higher standard of righteousness through the grace and light of His Son.

DOES GOD STILL OVERLOOK DIVORCE?

"And they said, Moses suffered to write a bill of divorcement, and to put her away. And Jesus answered and said unto them, For the hardness of your heart he wrote you this precept. But from the beginning of the creation God made them male and female. For this cause shall a man leave his father and mother, and cleave to his wife; and they twain shall be one flesh: so then they are no more twain, but one flesh. What therefore God hath joined together, let not man put asunder" (Mark 10:4-9).

In responding to the Pharisees, Jesus pointed to the root problem in troubled marriages—hard hearts. He also hinted at the weakness of the Mosaic dispensation. Under Moses, numerous practices fell beneath the ideal. This was a preparatory dispensation, and as Paul said at Athens, "The times of this ignorance God winked at" (Acts 17:30). Jesus made it very clear, however, that what God had permitted under Moses was no longer acceptable.

Divorce indicates a heart problem, but it does not solve that heart problem. It only bypasses it. Under the New Covenant, hardhearted husbands and wives can be given new hearts by the transforming power of the Spirit. Jesus the heartchanger has come, and God's standards for marriage can be restored to His intention "from the beginning." Certainly, the new birth does not automatically solve all marriage problems, but it does deal with the hard heart from which marriage problems arise, and it does open us to God's provisions for solving those problems. In the age of the Spirit, therefore, God commands, "Let not man put asunder."

HOW DO PEOPLE JUSTIFY DIVORCE TODAY?

1. People justify divorce today by misinterpreting God's grace.

A very common line of reasoning used nowadays by people trying to justify divorce is that we live in an age of grace. Apparently, to such, this means that God overlooks disobedience more now than He did under the Law. He isn't quite as strict as He used to be, and therefore, even though He may not want people to divorce, He will kindly look the other way.

This surely represents a misunderstanding of

grace. The New Testament does teach grace, and grace surely is the basis for our forgiveness. The Apostle Paul writes, "Where sin abounded, grace did much more abound" (Romans 5:20), assuring us that God's grace is greater, broader, deeper than our sin, and we can rest in His forgiveness.

Such assurances, however, are not intended to make us careless or bold to sin, for Paul hastens to ask, "What shall we say then? Shall we continue in sin, that grace may abound? God forbid. How shall we, that are dead to sin, live any longer therein?" (Romans 6:1, 2). God's grace is sufficient to forgive us our sins and to get us out of sin, but it is not intended to give us freedom to continue in sin.

To presume so upon the grace of God today is worse than to presume upon the Law of Moses. "He that despised Moses' law died without mercy under two or three witnesses: Of how much sorer punishment, suppose ye, shall he be thought worthy, who hath trodden under foot the Son of God, and hath counted the blood of the covenant, wherewith he was sanctified, an unholy thing, and hath done despite unto the Spirit of grace? For we know him that hath said, Vengeance belongeth unto me, I will recompense, saith the Lord. And again, The Lord shall judge his people. It is a fearful thing to fall into the hands of the living God" (Hebrews 10:28-31).

Is not this passage very clear? Those who presumptuously disregard what Jesus the Son of God says are worse off than those who disregarded what Moses said. Jesus said clearly, "What therefore God hath joined together, let not man put asunder" (Mark 10:9). People who get a divorce are not magnifying the grace of God by their willful disobedience to Jesus' teaching. They are despising that grace. They are, as Jude wrote, "turning the grace of our God into lasciviousness [shameless immorality]" (Jude 4). Grace teaches us to deny ungodliness and worldly lusts (Titus 2:12).

2. People justify divorce today by following popular practice.

So many today are divorcing their partners that it seems increasingly justifiable on the basis of common practice alone. Furthermore, there are church members and ministers in nearly all denominations who are involved in divorce. With so many people, so many professing Christians, and so many among our own acquaintances involved in divorce, there is tremendous pressure to conform to popular thinking about this issue. To follow what Jesus taught means taking a very unpopular position. It means exposure to pressure, misunderstanding, accusation, and ridicule.

The bottom line for what is right or wrong, however, is not what others are doing, but what God has said. God has said clearly that divorce is wrong. Therefore, marriage for life is right no matter if nobody does it, and divorce is wrong no matter if everybody does it.

3. People justify divorce today by reasoning that they are victims.

Most people end up saying, "I didn't want a divorce, but . . . I had no other choice." To be sympathetic and understanding here, we must recognize that marriage problems can be very complex and extremely painful. There are no easy answers to these problems. When marriage problems multiply, divorce often looks like the only way out, like an answer that normally wouldn't be considered but has to be under the circumstances.

Hard as this may sound, such thinking is the reasoning of the flesh. It is the reasoning of the serpent in the garden of Eden. Disobedience to God should not be considered a valid option for resolving man's problems. Saul tried "victim reasoning" when he was caught offering a sacrifice— a work only the priests were to do. He said, "Because I saw that the people were scattered from me, and that thou camest not within the days appointed, and that the Philistines gathered themselves together . . . I forced myself therefore, and offered a burnt offering" (I Samuel 13:11, 12). He tried it again when he disobeyed God's directions concerning Amalek. Samuel replied, "To obey is better than sacrifice, and to hearken than the fat of rams. For rebellion is as the sin of witchcraft, and stubbornness is as iniquity and idolatry" (I Samuel 15:22, 23).

Because God has clearly forbidden divorce as a means of solving marriage problems, we must not consider it as a valid option, no matter who does it. There are other options for those who are willing to look in faith to God. Furthermore, we serve a God who can part the seas, who can calm the storm, who can raise up and cast down, who holds the power of life and death, and who takes the cause of the meek, the poor, and the needy as His very own. "All my bones shall say, LORD, who is like unto thee, which deliverest the poor from him that is too strong for him, yea, the poor and the needy from him that spoileth him? . . . For he shall stand at the right hand of the poor, to save him from those that condemn his soul" (Psalm 35:10; 109:31).

Those who divorce because they believe they have no other choice are not acting in faith. Like Saul, they are saying, "I had no choice, God, but to disobey You." Unfortunately, they are shutting their lives off from the blessing and help of heaven and turning instead to the ways and methods of man.

4. People justify divorce by listening to popular, humanistic psychology.

We are taught by humanistic thinking today that personal satisfaction is everyone's right. Everybody deserves the privilege of living as happily and as free from trouble as possible, and everybody deserves the chance to develop his own inherent potential to the full. Where a bad marriage, a miserable partner, or "traditional values" stand in the way of personal happiness and fulfillment, these things are considered evil, and people are led to believe they are justified in removing them. Nobody should have to live with a scoundrel the rest of his life just because of a hasty, immature decision.

We could wish that Christians would not succumb to such thinking. In reality, however, some unwitting persons buy it in full, and others are influenced by it far too much.

Again, as Christians we must be understanding. Some people make horrendous mistakes in choosing a marriage partner. To remain in their marriage for life means they may suffer. Things will never be as they might have been. But those who obey Jesus can walk through their pain and deprivation with One who is intimately acquainted with human sorrows. Jesus can bear the yoke with them. And He can turn their wrecked lives into powerful messages of His grace and goodness.

Such concepts are beyond the realm of the humanistic psychologists. They are understood only by the obedient followers of Jesus. They are for those who hunger and thirst after righteousness more than any earthly pleasure or satisfaction, for those who desire holiness and the knowledge of God more than life itself.

  5. People justify divorce today by misinterpret-

Matthew records Jesus as saying, "Whosoever shall put away his wife, saving for the cause of fornication, causeth her to commit adultery: and whosoever shall marry her that is divorced committeth adultery" (Matthew 5:32). And again, "Whosoever shall put away his wife, except it be for fornication, and shall marry another, committeth adultery: and whoso marrieth her which is put away doth commit adultery" (Matthew 19:9).

Both verses have a similar exception—"saving for the cause of fornication" and "except it be for fornication." This exception has been made the center of much controversy, particularly by people who have tried to find justification for divorce and remarriage. In recognition of the many wars that have been waged on this small plot of Scripture and the marriages which could be preserved if people indeed followed Jesus' words, we will spend some time discussing this exception clause. Even so, we will need to summarize and simplify the mass of artillery and technical weaponry which scholars have unleashed over these few words.

Consider the following points:

a. The exception refers to the putting away. Note its placement in both verses. The order of the phrases is the same in the Greek as in the English—the "if not for fornication" (literal rendering) is an adverbial phrase modifying the preceding verb *apoluo*—"put away." Does this mean a

29

person may put away an unfaithful marriage partner? We will return to this question after we have noted more about these verses.

b. Matthew 5:32 and 19:9 vary in what they say after the exception.

—5:32 ". . . causeth her to commit adultery." A divorced woman commits adultery if she begins another relationship, but her husband is guilty of causing this sin by putting her away.

—19:9 ". . . and shall marry another committeth adultery." Any new relationship following a putting away is adulterous.

c. Mark and Luke include no exception. "Whosoever shall put away his wife, and marry another, committeth adultery against her. And if a woman shall put away her husband, and be married to another, she committeth adultery" (Mark 10:11, 12). "Whosoever putteth away his wife, and marrieth another, committeth adultery: and whosoever marrieth her that is put away from her husband committeth adultery" (Luke 16:18). Notice that in Mark the prohibition against divorce and remarriage is given to the woman as well as to the man.

d. Paul forbade departing from a marriage partner, forbade remarriage, and encouraged reconciliation if separation did occur. What is significant about this point is that this writing may well have been the earliest New Testament writing on the subject. The date for the earliest Gospels (Matthew and Mark) is commonly set in the middle or late 50s (or early 60s); Paul wrote I Corinthians around 55 A.D. But whether Paul was the first to record Jesus' teaching on marriage or second or third, he obviously knew Jesus' teaching well.

"And unto the married I command, yet not I, but the Lord, Let not the wife depart from her husband: But and if she depart, let her remain unmarried, or be reconciled to her husband: and let not the husband put away his wife" (I Corinthians 7:10, 11). In verse 11 he implies that separation may at times occur. Some feel this refers to the exception Jesus gave. In any case, Paul is clear that if there is separation, there is to be no remarriage while one's partner is living, but reconciliation if possible.

e. Jesus' teaching shows that marriage is indissoluble. The marriage bond cannot be broken by "putting away." This is unmistakable because Jesus referred to any subsequent relationship, either for the one put away or for the one who puts away, as adultery. This was new to the Jews. They understood divorce to completely sever the marriage bond. "And when she is departed out of his house, she may go and be another man's wife" (Deuteronomy 24:2). The "writing of divorcement" stated clearly that the wife was "free at thy own disposal, to marry whomsoever thou pleasest, without hindrance from anyone, from this day for ever."[1] For Jesus to call such remarriage adultery was startling to them. Even the disciples

31

responded, "If the case of the man be so with his wife, it is not good to marry" (Matthew 19:10). If there is no backing out of the marriage bond, in other words, maybe it's better never to marry.

f. Paul records the same understanding that death and death only severs the marriage bond. Any other relationship during this marriage is adultery. "The woman which hath an husband is bound by the law to her husband so long as he liveth; but if the husband be dead, she is loosed from the law of her husband. So then if, while her husband liveth, she be married to another man, she shall be called an adulteress: but if her husband be dead, she is free from that law; so that she is no adulteress, though she be married to another man" (Romans 7:2, 3).

g. Jesus' teaching shows that man's laws are at times at variance with God's laws. What man does to divide a marriage does not sever the bond in God's sight. What man calls remarriage, in God's eyes is adultery if the true partner is still living.

h. The early church leaders understood Jesus to teach that remarriage was adultery. Jerome, for example, wrote, "A husband may be an adulterer or a sodomite, he may be stained with every crime and may have been left by his wife because of his sins; yet he is still her husband, and, so long as he lives, she may not marry another."[2]

The innocent party idea came from Erasmus, a humanist theologian at the time of the Reformation. Luther and Calvin, as well as other

Reformation leaders, swallowed Erasmus's ideas kernel and hull. They were perhaps susceptible to the false idea because their Catholic opponents claimed the historic position—lifetime faithfulness in marriage, no remarriage—but the handling of marriage affairs by Catholic authorities was rife with abuses.

As we have shown, the exception qualifies Jesus' statement on putting away. It was not understood by the Apostles or the early church leaders to give permission to remarry. Although the Old Testament writing of divorce did include the freedom to remarry, Jesus said that from the beginning it was not so. He restored God's original order, declaring that remarriage while one's partner is still living is adultery.

But now again, does the exception permit divorce for marital unfaithfulness?

WHAT DOES THE "EXCEPTION CLAUSE" MEAN?

"Whosoever shall put away his wife, saving for the cause of fornication, causeth her to commit adultery: and whosoever shall marry her that is divorced committeth adultery" (Matthew 5:32). "Whosoever shall put away his wife, except it be for fornication, and shall marry another, committeth adultery: and whoso marrieth her which is put away doth commit adultery" (Matthew 19:9).

Unfortunately, seeing the exception as referring to the "putting away" does not resolve all controversy. But fortunately, the differences are relatively minor. They center largely around the meaning of the word translated "fornication." The Greek word is *porneia*. This word can have a rather broad meaning of immorality and sexual misconduct in general, or it can have more specific usages, such as fornication or whoredom (that is, prostitution—the root *porn* means "to sell").

Some scholars have understood *porneia* to mean strictly fornication, that is, sexual relations before marriage. They would understand Jesus to be making a comment on Jewish espousal custom.

Since this view has had wide acceptance among conservative people, we will consider it rather carefully. The Jewish betrothal was begun with a proposal and a commitment made in the presence of witnesses. It was beyond the private promise made in modern engagements, and was considered legally binding. Furthermore, espoused partners were referred to as husband and wife (see Matthew 1:19 and 20—"Joseph her husband" and "Mary thy wife"). Therefore to break an espousal in Jewish society required a legal separation—a writing of divorcement equivalent to that required of married couples.

According to this view, Jesus' exception was aimed primarily at this Jewish situation. He was saying, in other words, that divorce is wrong, except the putting away of an espoused partner who is unfaithful during engagement.

Joseph was in such a predicament when he learned that Mary his espoused "wife" was with child. "Then Joseph her husband, being a just man, and not willing to make her a publick example, was minded to put her away privily" (Matthew 1:19). Those who hold the espousal view see Joseph's contemplated action as an example of what Jesus had in mind when He said, "saving for the cause of fornication." They insist further that while the term *porneia* has a broader meaning at times, it means "fornication" strictly (sexual relations before marriage) when used with the term *moichao* (adultery), as in these passages. Certainly, the only time a "wife" could possibly commit "fornication" would be during the betrothal period.

Another pillar of support for this position is that Matthew alone includes this exception. Matthew wrote his Gospel particularly with the Jewish people in mind. The Jewish audience would readily understand this exception for fornication.

The major premises of the espousal view would be as follows:

a. Jesus did away with the Mosaic provision for divorcement.

b. Marriage, therefore, is for life.

c. Remarriage while one's partner is still living constitutes adultery.

d. To the Jews, Jesus qualified His no divorce

position: Putting away an espoused wife for fornication during espousal is an exception to His statement against putting away.

While this understanding is certainly compatible with Jesus' major position (no divorce, no remarriage), we would note that no early church writer understood this as referring to the Jewish betrothal period. This would not automatically negate the espousal view, for the early writers misunderstood Jesus elsewhere, too. They did know ancient Greek, however, with a fluency no modern scholar can equal. How did these early writers understand the exception clause?

The ante-Nicene fathers did not understand *porneia* as "fornication," strictly speaking, but as "whoredom," or persistent unfaithfulness. Jesus was not making an exception for an adulterous affair, or He would have used the word for adultery, *moichao*. Instead, He used *porneia*, indicating a promiscuous partner. Jesus was saying, in other words: no divorce, no remarriage; excepting, a man may put away his wife if she persists in sexual unfaithfulness. He need not continue, in other words, living in a three-way relationship. The early church writers in the second and third centuries almost universally taught this position.

To understand the early church position, we need to realize that their understanding of "put away" was not necessarily synonymous with modern divorce. Modern divorce, like Moses' "writing of divorcement," is a legal process which includes the legal right to remarry. The early church understood clearly that that kind of divorcement, though granted by Moses, was done away by Christ. To divorce in the sense of severing the union and permitting remarriage was not permitted in the early church.

To "put away" a companion, to them, meant literally to "send forth" or to "leave." This was more a physical process than a legal process, and thus would be more the equivalent of separation than of modern divorce. In Roman society, "putting away" actually required no legal process. The early church understood that Jesus' exception meant a Christian companion could "put away" a promiscuous companion. If a man had a wife, in other words, who cohabited with other men—who practiced whoredom rather than faithful love—he could "put her away." That is, he could either send her out or he himself could leave.

Since Jesus did away with Mosaic divorcement, the early church understood that to put away a companion for whoredom meant one of two things: either singlehood or reconciliation. Remarriage was not an option.

This position is consistent with the way God related to Israel. He called for their faithful devotion. But when they turned to idols, He withdrew His presence, not to seek someone else, but to wait until repentance on their part brought them back to His love.

Let's summarize the basic premises of the early

church position:
- a. Jesus set aside the Mosaic provision for divorcement (which likewise forbids the modern equivalent—divorce).
- b. Thus, marriage is for life.
- c. Remarriage while one's companion is still living constitutes adultery.
- d. Putting away a companion is wrong, excepting putting away a promiscuous companion. (The modern equivalent of putting away a promiscuous companion as taught by the early church would be separating and remaining single.)

Early church writers in the second, third, and fourth centuries could have been wrong in their understanding of the exception clause. Perhaps, as the espousal view maintains, Jesus made the exception for a specific Jewish audience, Matthew alone recording it. As we noted earlier, the espousal view is consistent with Jesus' basic position: no divorce, no remarriage. The early church view is likewise consistent with this basic position. Although they did permit putting away for whoredom, they understood Jesus to have set aside divorce in the Mosaic sense (and thus in the modern sense also). Marriage is for life—no exception.[3]

WHY DO MODERN TRANSLATIONS RENDER THE MEANING OF *PORNEIA* AS

"UNCHASTITY"?

Modern translators tend to translate *porneia* in the exception according to the view of Erasmus. Thus the NASB reads "unchastity" in Matthew 5:32 and "immorality" in 19:9. The NIV reads "marital unfaithfulness" in both cases. These translations are despite the fact that lexicons commonly render the word *porneia* as "fornication" or "whoredom."

The fallacy of translating *porneia* as general "unchastity" in these verses is especially evident when we examine the context. Consider the following points:

1. If Jesus meant adultery (as "unchastity," "immorality," and "marital unfaithfulness" all imply), He surely would have used the term for adultery— moichao. He was not using terms carelessly, especially in disputing with legal experts.

2. The "unchastity" translations cause Jesus to say what would have sided Him with one of the factions of the Pharisees. In Matthew 19, the Pharisees were trying to draw Jesus into a controversy they had among themselves. (They asked their question, "tempting him.") One side followed a liberal teacher named Hillel, who allowed divorce for virtually any reason. The other side followed stricter Shammai, who allowed divorce only for marital unfaithfulness. Jesus followed neither.

He said, "What therefore God hath joined together, let not man put asunder" (Matthew 19:6); that is, "No divorce" (equivalent to saying, "I don't agree with either of you").The Pharisees objected. If Jesus had then changed His statement to mean, "No divorce, except for marital unfaithfulness," He would have been backing down from His original statement (equivalent to saying, "I agree with Shammai").

3. *Such a position would have occasioned no surprise from Jesus' disciples.* They exclaimed (after His exception), "If the case of the man be so with his wife, it is not good to marry" (Matthew 19:10). If Jesus had merely been confirming Shammai's position (no divorce except for marital unfaithfulness), why would they think His teaching was so radical? Jesus clearly was teaching a position with which even the disciples were unfamiliar.

4. *The "unchastity" translations do not agree with Luke and Mark,* who both clearly understood Jesus' teaching to be: Marriage for life; no divorce, no remarriage, period.

We conclude that the modern translations present a mistranslation of *porneia* in Matthew 5:32 and 19:9. The meaning of *porneia* is required by the context to mean something more restrictive than general unchastity, something other than adultery, something which allows Jesus' teaching on lifelong marriage to cause surprise to Jesus' disciples.

Understandably, translators are not to be expositors. They should not insert clarifications into the text. The restrictive meaning of "fornication," however, as the KJV renders *porneia*, is more faithful to the context than the words used in modern translations. "Whoredom" would be a restrictive rendering in keeping with the understanding of the early church.

WHY IS DIVORCE WRONG?

In the book *Christian Family Living* seven reasons are given in answer to this question. Because they speak to the point and summarize much of what has been said here, we quote them in full:

1. Divorce is against the clear Word of God. "What therefore God hath joined together, let not man put asunder" (Mark 10:9).

2. Divorce is against the character of God. In Malachi 2, God calls divorce "treachery." God is faithful. What He promises, He does. Divorce is all in contrast to the faithful character of God. Love calls for loyalty. Those who divorce betray this sacred commitment of love, demonstrating, instead, unfaithfulness and treachery. The impact of Malachi 2, however, is not primarily broken marriage vows, but Israel's broken covenant with God. In graphic language, God demonstrated that

41

covenant breakers with men become covenant breakers with God. Where the spirit of treachery is in human relationships, in other words, it will be in one's relationship with God. Small wonder that God says, "I hate putting away."

3. Divorce demonstrates hardness of heart. Jesus frankly said divorce was permitted for "hardness of . . . heart" (Mark 10:5). To this could be added the witness of many marriage counselors. The underlying problem in marital conflict is self-centeredness. Divorce is but the continued expression of a hard heart. It takes humility, love, and brokenness to resolve marriage problems and to experience the oneness intended in marriage.

4. Divorce hurts one's partner. Treachery is a betrayal word. Where there is betrayal, there is hurt. Trust and loyalty are intrinsically bound up in love, and divorce knifes mercilessly through those bonds causing hurt. Always. It is impossible to divorce a legitimate relationship between man and woman as an act of love and compassion. Attitudes of hate and hurt are always present.

5. Divorce hurts children and scars their lives. Following is the testimony of one daughter whose parents divorced:

"Please, please don't sign them! O Daddy, don't sign those papers!" My pleadings must have added greatly to my father's burden, but the pen held firmly in his hand continued to write his name on the final paper.

Thus was my world destroyed and I with it, for on that day something died in the heart of a child. . . .

Bitter protests and tears were vain, for divorce courts do not consider human hearts when they collect their dues. Mother and Daddy were to be "free," but we children were not. I became a slave to despair. The quarrels? They ceased, to be sure, but cries of heartbroken children took their place, and I for one, longed to hear those quarrels if only it meant I could have my mother and daddy back! . . .

I wish I could take the hand of every parent harboring the thought of divorce, and lead you back with me into the valley through which I have come. If the hurt of an innocent child's heart, the bitter shock of a tender life, the tears of the unwanted, misplaced child, the horror and gloom could be called to witness in the divorce courts, no child would again have to walk the dreadful road that starts with the signing of those final papers in the divorce courts. Instead, the tears would become your own and in the valley you would realize that the ones who suffer in divorce and remarriage are the innocent children.[4]

6. Divorce creates further barriers to reconciliation. In his first letter to the Corinthians, Paul warns against even separating from an unbelieving partner, but then says, "If she depart, let her remain unmarried, or be reconciled to her husband: and let not the husband put away his wife" (I Corinthians 7:11). While we are not discussing separation here, we can readily see that Paul instructs towards reconciliation, not away from it, even with unbelieving partners. And he also implies that divorce is like adding a padlock to the door through which an unfaithful partner has gone. Where reconciliation is the objective, divorce cannot be an option.

7. Divorce perpetuates sin.

People choose divorce as an answer to their marriage problems. But it is impossible to correct problems through disobedience to God. Divorce always creates more problems. Jesus noted specifically that divorce is a cause of adultery (Matthew 5:32). No one can keep the consequences of sin to himself, and this seems especially true with divorce. Sin leads to sins, and those sins multiply in the generations to come. Studies have shown that those who come from divorced homes have a higher rate of divorce than those whose parents remained faithful. Sin simply snowballs.[5]

WHAT ARE SOME PRACTICAL SUGGES-
TIONS FOR THOSE IN DIFFICULT
MARRIAGES?

If divorce is not an option what alternatives are there when a couple is having severe marriage problems—when, for example, a partner is abusive, or when a partner is immoral, or when a partner is involved in illegal activities, or when a non-Christian partner is drawing the children into sinful activities?

These situations ought never to be viewed lightly. Because circumstances vary considerably, it would be impossible to provide specific guidance for all situations. There are Biblical principles and directives, however, which can be applied in very practical and specific ways.

1. In a difficult marriage, a Christian must be committed to honoring the Biblical roles for husband and wife.

"Wives, submit yourselves unto your own husbands, as unto the Lord. Husbands, love your wives, even as Christ also loved the church, and gave himself for it" (Ephesians 5:22, 25).

A husband is called to a role of loving headship in the home. A wife is called to support and submit to her husband. In a marriage that is crumbling on the verge of divorce, there is usually a breakdown somewhere in responsibility. Indeed, one prime source of trouble in the home is a domineering husband or wife. A Christian husband should attend carefully to the Biblical teaching for husbands, and a wife to the teaching for wives. A husband or wife in a troubled marriage may find it helpful to make a list of personal responsibilities, number them in order of priority, and then discuss this list with his or her companion, noting suggestions for improvement. Certainly, heartfelt love is a better motivation in marriage than a checklist, but a checklist may be a helpful step in restoring love.

2. In a difficult marriage, a Christian needs the security and support of a faithful brotherhood.

"Whether one member suffer, all the members suffer with it; or one member be honoured, all the members rejoice with it" (I Corinthians 12:26).

Any member of Christ's body should have the security that when he is in trouble, his brothers and sisters understand, empathize, and stand ready to provide care as needed.

This verse taken in context would indicate there are some sufferings which God does not intend that we bear alone, sufferings which actually require the support of the larger body. Unfortunately, people who are having marriage problems often find the problems so traumatic, so painful, and so personal that they do not want to share them with anyone. They want to isolate themselves. There certainly is a place for privacy—personal problems need not always become common knowledge to all members in the church. On the other hand, a mature body of believers can provide a prayer support, a caring, and a togetherness in trial which is invaluable to suffering members. The more a brotherhood practices mutual love, trust, openness, and humility, the easier it will be for hurting members to seek the support and care of the larger body.

3. In a difficult marriage, a Christian should seek the counsel of spiritually mature husbands and wives.

> "The aged men be sober, grave, temperate, sound in faith, in charity, in patience. The aged women likewise, that they be in behaviour as becometh holiness, not false accusers, not given to much wine, teachers of good things; that they may teach the young women to be sober, to love their husbands, to love their children, to be discreet, chaste, keepers at home, good, obedient to their own husbands, that the word of God be not blasphemed. Young men likewise exhort to be sober minded" (Titus 2:2-6).

This Scripture clearly guides the younger to learn from the more mature those down-to-earth duties of married life. The unfortunate neglect of this teaching ministry in most churches is no doubt in part the cause of the breakdown in many marriages. A generation ago, men and women were forsaking the roles God had ordained for marriage. The present generation has not only many marriage problems, but also in too many settings they have few older couples who are able to help them correct their problems and order their homes. The mindset of the day is "go see a marriage counselor." Too many marriage counselors, unfortunately, have been trained in procedures which reject the counsel of God.

An apostate church setting, then, undermines the effectiveness of this approach to marriage problems. There still are churches, however, where the integrity of marriage has been maintained and where the older are able to teach the younger the nitty-gritty of married life. This is God's plan.

4. In a difficult marriage, a Christian should take up the responsibility of rebuilding the marriage as far as possible.

"And unto the married I command, yet not I, but the Lord, Let not the wife depart from her husband: But and if she depart, let her remain unmarried, or be reconciled to her husband: and let not the husband put away his wife" (I Corinthians 7:10, 11).

As we saw earlier, in the Old Testament God permitted divorce under certain circumstances. Divorce granted the privilege to marry another but forbade returning to the former partner. In the New Testament, however, Jesus reinstituted God's original purpose and not only forbade divorce but said if one does divorce and marries another, he commits adultery—the first marriage still stands in God's sight. Paul instructed believers, therefore, not to depart from their companions, but if they departed to remain unmarried or be reconciled.

Since marriage is indissoluble, those who are separated or divorced are called to the work of reconciliation—restoring the relationship and rebuilding the marriage as much as is within their power. Seeing oneself as a rebuilder can bring a whole new dimension to a difficult marriage. It brings purpose. It is altogether reversed from the victim perspective.

How does one go about rebuilding?

There are seven basic areas where the rebuilding needs to take place:

- Relationship with God.
- Relationship with oneself.
- Relationship with one's spouse.
- Relationship with the children.
- Relationship with the extended family.
- Relationship with the church.
- Testimony of righteousness.

The rebuilder should develop goals in each of

these areas, acknowledging where he is in relation to where God wants him to be and projecting realistic steps to arrive there. Using a pencil and paper can be helpful in listing specific goals and steps. A trusted person who can serve as a spiritual guide can offer invaluable help as well. Let's consider each area briefly.

a. Rebuild a relationship with God. The rebuilder needs to seek the Lord daily to experience the purity of soul and the courage to face the difficulties of rebuilding his marriage. Daily fellowship with God not only strengthens and purifies the spirit, but it also keeps the rebuilder aware of his need to rely on God. "Except the LORD build the house, they labour in vain that build it" (Psalm 127:1). "For the eyes of the LORD run to and fro throughout the whole earth, to shew himself strong in the behalf of them whose heart is perfect toward him" (II Chronicles 16:9).

b. Rebuild a relationship with oneself. One of the greatest areas of conflict in a difficult marriage is the inner conflict in one's own heart and mind. This conflict is often subconscious. It revolves much around the unfulfilled longing for love and security and the nagging consciousness of failure. A proper relationship with oneself requires being in touch with one's real thoughts and feelings.

It requires being honest. And often it requires being open with a mature friend to discuss these inner feelings. Reading the Psalms can help one toward this inner honesty. Inner peace comes further as the broken and contrite one allows the Lord to renew a right spirit and rebuild character qualities such as meekness, compassion, faith, temperance, gentleness, and godliness. Consider the Beatitudes (Matthew 5) for steps to rebuilding an inner peace.

c. Rebuild a relationship with one's spouse. This may have its limitations. The spouse may have left, may even have remarried. According to I Corinthians 7:15, the believing partner in such a case is to let the unbeliever depart. Nonetheless, to the extent that he can, the rebuilder should clear up all past failures and sins against his partner. He should further open himself to hearing his spouse's viewpoint, listening without justification, trying to see it from his spouse's perspective. He should refuse to belittle or condemn his spouse either in his own mind or to others. If there are injustices, he should choose to respond according to the teaching of Jesus: "Bless them that curse you, do good to them that hate you, and pray for them which despitefully use you, and persecute you" (Matthew 5:44).

d. Rebuild a relationship with the children.
God intends that fathers and mothers be
involved in teaching and training their children in His ways. "And these words, which I
command thee this day, shall be in thine
heart: And thou shalt teach them diligently
unto thy children, and shalt talk of them
when thou sittest in thine house, and when
thou walkest by the way, and when thou liest
down, and when thou risest up"
(Deuteronomy 6:6, 7). Children further need
the nurturing and caring, the correction and
discipline, and the love and provision of their
parents. Where separation has already
occurred, this will be more limited, but the
rebuilder must take whatever steps he can in
the responsibility of loving his children and
training them in the ways of God.

*e. Rebuild a relationship with the extended
family.* Most marriage problems spill out into
the larger family. Alienation, hurts, and misunderstanding on the broader scale con-
tribute to the problems in the marriage relationship. A rebuilder needs to take down the
walls and rebuild the bridges so that the
extended family is working together and
praying together toward the restoration of
the marriage. Even as pride often lies at the
bottom of conflict, so humility is often the
key to rebuilding. A rebuilder may need to

confess his faults in brokenness and humility to rebuild such relationships, but it is that very humility which releases God's grace. "God resisteth the proud, and giveth grace to the humble" (I Peter 5:5).

f. Rebuild a relationship with the church. We noted earlier that the rebuilder needs a solid relationship with a mature brotherhood to bear the burden of a difficult marriage. The brotherhood, on the other hand, needs the testimony and ministry of those who choose to live for God in difficult situations. Sometimes people in difficult marriages believe they are being a burden to the church because they need so much prayer, encouragement, and help. In reality, however, the church needs every member who seeks after God. "Nay, much more those members of the body, which seem to be more feeble, are necessary" (I Corinthians 12:22). Furthermore, the church can often supply the counsel and support for difficult decisions a person faces in working through a tangled marriage situation. "Where no counsel is, the people fall: but in the multitude of counsellors there is safety" (Proverbs 11:14).

g. Rebuild a testimony of righteousness. The rebuilder needs a clear testimony of righteousness. Everyone knows that marriage conflicts are unpleasant, but few people, especially among the ungodly, know that the commitment to work through tough marriage problems is a better choice than the practice of breaking commitments. When those involved in conflict, separation, or divorce are seen cooperating with God in the difficult task of rebuilding, their lives trumpet a testimony of God's grace. There ARE alternatives to divorce. There IS a way to restore broken relationships. There ARE right ways of coping with very difficult human problems.

AS A CHRISTIAN WHO HAS EXPERIENCED DIVORCE, HOW DO I COPE WITH REJECTION?

Wrong as divorce is, some believers experience it. They may have been divorced against their will. Or they may have initiated the divorce prior to conversion or in a state of disobedience, and came to the willingness to rebuild their marriage after the damage of divorce has been done.

Painless divorce is impossible. Two hearts so gladly united in love are ripped apart. Out of the wound erupt questions that have no answers, replies that cannot be put into words, feelings too poignant for sense, and loneliness unimagined. In this emotional maelstrom are a thousand points of pain, each distinct from the other, each demanding examination and treatment, but all screaming one inescapable message: REJECTION!

No one who has been divorced can escape the pain of rejection. If the sense of rejection cannot be avoided, how can one cope with it? There are at least three things necessary for the Christian in such a situation.

1. Be honest about personal responsibility in the former relationship.

> "If we walk in the light, as he is in the light, we have fellowship one with another, and the blood of Jesus Christ his Son cleanseth us from all sin. If we say that we have no sin, we deceive ourselves, and the truth is not in us. If we confess our sins, he is faithful and just to forgive us our sins, and to cleanse us from all unrighteousness" (I John 1:7-9).

A part of any Christian's ability to handle rejection is being willing to be honest with God and oneself, to acknowledge clearly one's sins and shortcomings, and to open oneself to purging and inner growth. Personal honesty in the emotional trauma of divorce, however, is difficult, to put it mildly. It usually requires the honest help of a trustworthy Christian friend or pastor.

2. Find the security of God's acceptance.

"Study to shew thyself approved unto God, a workman that needeth not to be ashamed, rightly dividing the word of truth" (II Timothy 2:15).

"He hath made us accepted in the beloved" (Ephesians 1:6).

"And ye are complete in him" (Colossians 2:10).

"When my father and my mother forsake me, then the LORD will take me up" (Psalm 27:10).

Rock-bottom needs are met in God. He never intends that a companion provide our complete personal security. The Christian who experiences the devastation of being cast out of another person's life and love has the potential of experiencing acceptance with God in ways indescribable.

God's acceptance does not take away all the pain of marital rejection, but it reverses the effect of that rejection. It floods earth's sorrows with heaven's joy and gives fresh meaning and purpose to life.

3. Avoid bitterness.

"Husbands, love your wives, and be not

bitter against them" (Colossians 3:19).

"Follow peace with all men, and holiness, without which no man shall see the Lord: Looking diligently lest any man fail of the grace of God; lest any root of bitterness springing up trouble you, and thereby many be defiled" (Hebrews 12:14, 15).

Bitterness follows hard on the heels of rejection. But any who give it lodging are harboring the worst of criminals. In the dark night of depression and discouragement, bitterness will stealthily bind the spirit, rob the inner life of joy and peace and love, slosh its wicked fuel over the whole life— over memories, problems, personalities, situations past and present—and light the whole scene with the fire of hell.

It takes faith to thwart bitterness effectively. "Above all, taking the shield of faith, wherewith ye shall be able to quench all the fiery darts of the wicked" (Ephesians 6:16). Faith chooses to acknowledge a sovereign God. Faith responds with an obedient yes to the direction of God. Faith receives heaven's responses to human needs. Faith changes the focus from the offender to the mighty DEFENDER. Thus, faith learns to rejoice in God and refuses to grovel in self-pity, blame, and resentment. Faith is the key to overcoming bitterness and rejection.

REMARRIAGE

WHAT DOES THE BIBLE SAY ABOUT REMARRIAGE AFTER DIVORCE?

"Whosoever shall put away his wife, and marry another, committeth adultery against her. And if a woman shall put away her husband, and be married to another, she committeth adultery" (Mark 10:11, 12).

"The woman which hath an husband is bound by the law to her husband so long as he liveth; but if the husband be dead, she is loosed from the law of her husband. So then if, while her husband liveth, she be married to another man, she shall be called an adulteress: but if her husband be dead, she is free from that law; so that she is no adulteress, though she be married to another man" (Romans 7:2, 3).

Jesus and Paul are both unmistakably clear—remarriage is wrong while one's partner lives. Divorce does not give the right to marry again. To remarry is to enter a relationship of adultery.

DOESN'T PAUL SAY THAT IF AN UNBE-LIEVING PARTNER DEPARTS, "A BROTHER OR A SISTER IS NOT UNDER BONDAGE IN SUCH CASES" (I CORINTHIANS 7:15)?

To understand this statement, we must consider the context. In this letter, Paul is answering questions posed by the Corinthians in a former letter to him (see I Corinthians 7:1). In this passage, Paul gives clear instructions that for married people, sexual relations are right and should not be withheld, except by mutual consent for short periods of time. He furthermore instructs that married couples should not separate, that if they are separated, they must not remarry someone else, but rather seek to be reconciled. Even when the partner is an unbeliever, there should not be separation, for the believer may be the means of bringing both the unbelieving partner and the children to salvation. Following this we have the verse concerning "not under bondage." "But if the unbelieving depart, let him depart. A brother or a sister is not under bondage in such cases: but God hath called us to peace" (I Corinthians 7:15).

"Not under bondage" is misconstrued by some to mean that if an unbeliever divorces a believer, the believer is free to remarry. If that were the case, Paul would be contradicting himself. He had just said, "But and if she depart, let her remain unmarried, or be reconciled to her husband: and let not the husband put away his wife" (v. 11).

The phrase "not under bondage" is given in the context of speaking about marital obligations—giving "due benevolence," not withholding sexual relations, remaining with an unbeliever, and sanctifying the unbelieving partner and the children. If the unbeliever departs, the believer is free to let him or her depart and should not feel guilty for obligations he cannot perform. The believer is not bound, in other words, to live in the same house with and perform marital duties toward an unwilling, unbelieving partner. Rather, "God has called us to peace."

DOES AN ADULTEROUS MARRIAGE NEED TO BE BROKEN, OR CAN THE COUPLE ASK FOR FORGIVENESS AND REMAIN TOGETHER?

Consider the following Scripture again:

"And he saith unto them, Whosoever shall put away his wife, and marry another, committeth adultery against her. And if a woman shall put away her husband, and be married to another, she committeth adultery" (Mark 10:11, 12).

Under the Old Testament, a bill of divorce granted the right to remarry. The remarriage was not considered adulterous because God recognized the divorce—He recognized divorce, not as approving it, but because of the hardness of their hearts (Mark 10:5). Jesus said, however, that to divorce and remarry was adulterous. The marriage of two eligible partners, in other words, is indissoluble until death.

The Greek verb tense translated "committeth adultery" in Matthew 5:32; 19:9; Mark 10:11, 12; and Luke 16:18 is *present continuous action*. It means "is committing adultery." The adultery is not in the past only. It began when the second relationship began and continues as long as the relationship continues—the remarriage is ongoing adultery against the former companion as long as that companion lives. Again, this was not so under Moses, but it is so under the teachings of Jesus.

The only conclusion which deals adequately with Jesus' teaching is the conclusion to separate the adulterous relationship. Those who wish to be cleansed of their sin must forsake it.

Both the Old Testament and the New are clear that to ask for forgiveness of sin and remain in it is presumptuous. God asks the people of Jeremiah's day the incredulous question, "Will ye steal, murder, and commit adultery . . . And come and stand before me in this house, which is called by my name, and say, We are delivered to do all these abominations?" (Jeremiah 7:9,10). When the Pharisees came to John wanting baptism but not wanting to leave their sin, John minced no words about their presumption. "O generation of vipers, who hath warned you to flee from the wrath to come? Bring forth therefore fruits meet for repentance [in other words, demonstrate your repentance by genuine sorrow for your sins and a willingness to forsake them] (Matthew 3:7, 8).

Would we suppose that a member of the Mafia could find forgiveness simply by asking God, "Please forgive me," but then continuing in his Mafia membership and activities? Wouldn't we say that to get right with God he would need to break his commitments to the Mafia and leave his sinful practices—no more stealing, murder, extortion, dishonesty, etc.? Supposing he didn't. What testimony would he give to the next man he blackmails, the next company executive he swindles, the next person he bumps off—"You know, I know it's wrong to do this to you, but I've been forgiven by the mercy and grace of Jesus, and I know He'll pardon me for it. He could forgive you too if you just ask him, before I pull the trigger." How would that be for a testimony?

But is it any less presumptuous to continue in what Jesus clearly called adultery and say, "I know it's wrong, but I'm in it now and I'm sure Jesus will forgive me"?

"He that covereth his sins shall not prosper: but whoso confesseth and forsaketh them shall have mercy" (Proverbs 28:13).

IS IT PROPER TO INITIATE A DIVORCE FROM AN UNSCRIPTURAL RELATIONSHIP OR SHOULD THERE SIMPLY BE A SEPARATION?

We should note first that relationships may be unscriptural in several ways. The Mosaic Law forbids incestuous marriages—brother to sister, son to mother or stepmother, uncle to niece, etc. Modern law likewise forbids some of these—brother to sister and son to mother, for example; but modern law permits some relationships which the Law of Moses forbade—marriage of in-laws, for example. And modern law is teetering on the brink of permitting homosexual marriages (they are recognized in some Scandinavian countries). Modern law likewise permits the relationship Jesus forbade—marriage of divorced individuals.

Is it then proper to file for divorce for any or all such relationships which God considers wrong?

Viewing divorce as a legal suit filed against an offender would seem to go against the teachings of both Jesus and Paul. "And if any man will sue thee at the law, and take away thy coat, let him have thy cloke also" (Matthew 5:40). "Dare any of you, having a matter against another, go to law before the unjust, and not before the saints? Now therefore there is utterly a fault among you, because ye go to law one with another" (I Corinthians 6:1, 7).

We would note that while the above Scriptures certainly have application to any legal proceedings, they are speaking primarily about economic affairs, not about sinful marriage relationships. Furthermore, most states now provide for "no-fault divorce," which is not suit filed against another as an offender, but is a process which severs the legal marriage relation and makes arrangements for division of property, rights, and responsibilities.

It would seem that if legal proceedings are right for severing any unscriptural relationships, they are right for severing all such relationships. If it is right, in other words, for a Christian to take legal proceedings to separate an incestuous relationship or a homosexual relationship, it is right to take legal proceedings to separate an adulterous relationship. It would be wrong, however, in any such situation for a Christian to sue for personal rights, to fight legal battles to protect personal property. "Why do ye not rather take wrong? why do ye not rather suffer yourselves to be defrauded?" (I Corinthians 6:7).

What is proper legal action for severing unlawful or adulterous relationships, however, should not be assumed for the marriage relationship, even with a promiscuous partner. As Paul wrote in I Corinthians 7:10, 11, lawful partners should not even separate (though if separation occurs, one should remain unmarried or be reconciled), but divorce is forbidden.

WHAT IF THE DIVORCE AND REMAR-RIAGE OCCURRED BEFORE ONE WAS SAVED?

"Marriage is honourable in all, and the bed undefiled: but whoremongers and adulterers God will judge" (Hebrews 13:4). "Know ye not that the unrighteous shall not inherit the kingdom of God? Be not deceived: neither fornicators, nor idolaters, nor adulterers, nor effeminate, nor abusers of themselves with mankind, nor thieves, nor covetous, nor drunkards, nor revilers, nor extortioners, shall inherit the kingdom of God. And such were some of you: but ye are washed, but ye are sanctified, but ye are justified in the name of the Lord Jesus, and by the Spirit of our God" (I Corinthians 6:9-11).

God recognizes the marriages of the ungodly, and He sees their marriage sins also and holds them accountable for them. To think that adultery is excused because it was entered before one was saved is to think wrongly. The sins we commit before we are saved may well have lingering effects after we are saved. Zacchaeus said, "If I have taken any thing from any man by false accusation, I restore him fourfold. And Jesus said unto him, This day is salvation come to this house" (Luke 19:8, 9). Salvation brings us to the place where we reckon with our sins. Where we have done wrong, we must make right to the extent we are able—we restore what we have stolen, we repair what we have broken, and we break off that in which we have been wrongly engaged.

John the Baptist confronted Herod for taking his brother Philip's wife. Without apology, he said, "It is not lawful for thee to have her" (Matthew 14:4). Notice, he did not say, "If you believe in Jesus, you can be forgiven for your relationship with your brother's wife, and then you may keep her." The only credible understanding of John's words is that Herod should put her away. We might note that this relationship fell under the forbidden marriages of the Old Testament (see Leviticus 18:16). According to Jesus, however, ANY remarriage while the former partner is living is forbidden.

Trying to make a distinction between what occurred before conversion and what occurs after runs us into the following problems:

1. It creates confusion and debate about when one was actually saved. Some say, "Well, I was going to church, but I don't know if I was really saved at the time." Others, "Well, I had made a commitment to Jesus when I was young, but I was backslidden." And still others, "Well, I was going to church, but no one ever told me this was wrong." The variations are endless.

2. It leaves an incorrect impression on the young

and unmarried. The reasoning is, "As long as I'm not a Christian when I do these things, I can just ask for forgiveness and go on from there."

3. It leaves an unclear testimony to the world. What credible witness against other adulterous relationships can a divorced/remarried couple give? Or for that matter, what minister would have credibility in speaking as John the Baptist did against the sins of the ungodly if he permits such things in his own congregation?

4. It sets up a double standard among believers. Suppose a divorced/remarried couple receives Christ and is taken into the church. At the same time another divorced/remarried couple, whose marriage problems occurred while they were members in another church, seeks membership with your church. Would you tell the one, "You're forgiven and may remain together," but the other, "You must separate"? Besides creating negative feelings within the church, such a position would create confusion for the onlooking world.

WHAT IF THE OTHER PARTNER INITIATED THE DIVORCE?

"Whosoever marrieth her that is put away from her husband committeth adultery" (Luke 16:18).

"Whoso marrieth her which is put away doth commit adultery. His disciples say unto him, If the case of the man be so with his wife, it is not good to marry. But he said unto them, All men cannot receive this saying, save they to whom it is given. For there are some eunuchs, which were so born from their mother's womb: and there are some eunuchs, which were made eunuchs of men: and there be eunuchs, which have made themselves eunuchs for the kingdom of heaven's sake" (Matthew 19:9-12).

Very clearly in Jesus' teaching, a second marriage is wrong both for the one who initiates the divorce and for the one who is divorced. For both partners, the first marriage stands in God's sight, and it is adulterous to begin another relationship.

The reaction of the disciples was that perhaps it is better not to marry. Jesus acknowledged that His standard for lifelong marriage is high. Not all people would receive this teaching, just as they would reject many of His other teachings. But this is the standard for those whose ears are tuned to His kingdom, who are willing to be His true disciples.

To obey Jesus in this matter means being willing to live singly. In some cases, it is possible to rebuild the relationship with the first partner, against whom the adultery was being committed. Where this is not realized, however, the now-single people should, according to the instructions of Jesus, give their lives to the work of building God's kingdom. The message from such a decision and from their single life should be: "I came to believe that I was violating God's standard for marriage. In obedience to Him I have left an adulterous relationship and entered a life of devotedness to Him. I trust Him to work out the details and meet the needs of my heart. I would rather live the rest of my life single in obedience to God than to be married in disobedience to Him." This would be a direct response to Jesus' statement, "There be eunuchs, which have made themselves eunuchs for the kingdom of heaven's sake" (Matthew 19:12).

There are those who object to the idea that some people should be required to live a single life. The thinking seems to be that if marriage is one's desire, it should be one's right. Both Jesus and Paul, however, (whose teachings we have been examining) have demonstrated that ultimate fulfillment is not in marriage but in being in the will of God. Furthermore, their lives testify to the power and blessing that can flow from a single life devoted to the kingdom of God. The point is not that singlehood is better than marriage or vice versa, but that obedience to God must be held above either singlehood or marriage. Only in God's will can we experience the satisfaction of God's blessing and grace. Disobedience to God in this matter, though it may bring temporary companionship, will bring God's reproofs and will bring ruin in the end.

WHAT IF THERE ARE CHILDREN?

This question poses a practical dilemma, for on the one hand there is sin in the adulterous relationship, and on the other there seems to be sin in the neglect and hurt of the children if the couple should decide to separate.

There is no direct Scripture stating just how this is to be handled. In the Book of Ezra, the people of Israel had begun to take wives of the heathen, contrary to God's direction. When they wished to repent of this, they were asked to separate from their wives and their children (see Chapters 9 and 10). We are not told exactly how they did this, or if there was any support or contact with them later, but likely, these women were sent back with their children to their parents' home. While there certainly are differences between that culture and ours, and between that situation and the present problem of divorce and remarriage, there is the similarity in that both represent marriages contrary to God's will. And we can be sure God was no less compassionate then than He is today, nor is He less desiring of holiness today among His people than He was in that day.

Two basic principles must be kept in focus in working out a solution. First, the adulterous relationship is wrong; it must be discontinued. God's Word is clear that adulterers "shall not inherit the kingdom of God" (I Corinthians 6:9). We might call this the principle of righteousness. Second, the children are eternal beings who need love and training in a godly home setting. This might be called the principle of responsibility. Somewhere in the practical working out of this difficult situation, the principles of righteousness and responsibility must be satisfied.

Every situation will have its variables, and therefore, obedience to God must be bathed in prayer. Some couples work out an arrangement where the husband continues to provide for the material needs and continues to relate to the children regularly, but lives in separate quarters. The wife, then, is responsible for the day-by-day care of the children, sometimes with the help of relatives. This has the advantages of a clear testimony and of a continued father image for the children, but it takes resolve and cooperation and needs the support of the church and the extended family.

Ideally, both partners should be working together in finding a solution. Unfortunately, these kinds of situations are seldom ideal. The further anyone goes down the path of disobedience from God's standards for marriage, the more entangled they become, and the more difficult it is to turn back to the path of obedience.

Obedience is possible, however, for those who are committed.

IF AN UNSCRIPTURAL RELATIONSHIP IS TERMINATED AND ONE PARTY NEVER HAS HAD A LEGITIMATE MARRIAGE, IS THAT PERSON FREE TO MARRY?

This question and the next one are very difficult questions to face. Situations can vary considerably. And no matter how thorough or meticulous we are in defining a valid marriage, new situations have a way of adding a twist we had not considered and must weigh carefully. In applying Scriptural principles to these situations, Christians have not always arrived at the same conclusions. When we face these questions in actual experience, therefore, we do best to draw from the wisdom of a spiritual brotherhood, rather than trusting personal conclusions alone. All that we do must be to the glory of God (I Corinthians 10:31). All we do must have the effect of edification in the brotherhood (Romans 15:2). All we do must be above reproach before a watching world (I Peter 2:12).

Before we look at the above question directly, we should review Jesus' definition of marriage and adultery. In God's sight when a single man marries a single woman, they are bound in marriage for life. Any relationship with any third partner while the two live is adultery and calls for repentance and a return to fidelity.

This was not so under Moses. Both divorce and remarriage were permitted, and a remarriage was considered a binding marriage (see Deuteronomy

24:2). Under the New Testament, however, Jesus said, "Whosoever shall put away his wife, and marry another, committeth adultery against her. And if a woman shall put away her husband, and be married to another, she committeth adultery" (Mark 10:11, 12). The second couple now, according to Jesus, has not formed a legitimate marriage bond but an adulterous union.

Suppose, for illustration, Joe, a single man, marries Sue, the divorced wife of Sam. In God's sight, Joe and Sue cannot form a legitimate marriage bond. No matter how legal their action is by the laws of the land, God says Sue is committing adultery against her lifelong husband Sam.

Now suppose Joe and Sue divorce. Here we are back to our question. Is Joe free to marry a single woman?

We just noted that God did not view Joe and Sue as legitimately married. He viewed Sue as committing adultery against Sam. Joe was party to Sue's adultery. So Joe has never formed a legitimate marriage bond. He has been an accomplice in an adulterous relationship. From the standpoint of marriage, then, we cannot say Joe was bound to Sue.

There are, however, more factors to consider than one's strict marital status when determining how "free" one is to marry. Although a person may not be disqualified from marriage by a former marriage bond, he may have other bonds and obligations which make marriage inappropriate.

73

Paul asks, "Know ye not that he which is joined to an harlot is one body? for two, saith he, shall be one flesh" (I Corinthians 6:16). Although the physical union is not a marriage bond, it is a physical bond. It is also an emotional bond. And it may be a procreative bond. THE MORE TANGLED THESE BONDS, THE MORE INAPPROPRIATE MARRIAGE WOULD BE.

Some people have been married, divorced, and remarried numerous times when they come to Christ. They may have had children by several partners, including some to whom they never were legally joined (cf. John 4:18). Some may have had bonds of sexual union with many, children by several, but marriage to none. Would it be wise to sweep all these tangles aside with a simple assertion, "Well, I never was legitimately married in God's sight" and go happily into marriage? Would not even the ungodly raise their eyebrows if a man became a Christian, left a long-term adulterous relationship (with children), and married a single woman from the church, under the blessing of the church? One's strict marital status is surely not the only thing to consider in such cases. Wouldn't it be right to conclude that a marriage may be wrong even if it is not strictly adulterous? Certainly, singlehood for Joe (divorced from Sue) is a safe and honorable position.

The way we view the "wrongness" of marriage in Joe's case, however, may depend somewhat on whether the marriage is being contemplated or has already occurred. It is one thing if Joe (in the former illustration) has left Sue and is contemplating marriage to Jane, a single woman. His former involvements may be considered tangled enough to make marriage to Jane both inappropriate and wrong. That wrongness would be greatly intensified if an anticipated marriage to Jane was an apparent factor in ending his relationship with Sue. Trading one wife for another is certainly not the way to find pardon and cleansing from an adulterous marriage. But suppose Joe and Jane are already married. Though they may look back and acknowledge they did wrong in getting married, their relationship is not wrong in the way that Joe and Sue's relationship was. Neither Joe nor Jane, in other words, have had a true marital union; neither is in violation of a lifelong obligation of fidelity to another marriage partner. The wrongness of Joe and Jane's marriage is analogous to the wrongness of many other marriages wherein the people made marital decisions contrary to God's will for them. This kind of wrongness does not free Joe and Jane from their lifelong obligations of marriage, nor anyone else who has made very wrong decisions entering marriage.

We might raise yet another twist to this, however. Let's go back to Joe marrying Sue (the divorced wife of Sam). Their "marriage," according to Jesus, is an adulterous union. But suppose Joe and Sue are saved, and in the process of repentance and trying to get their lives straightened out, they learn that Sam (Sue's husband) has passed away. Does their adulterous relationship automatically become a legitimate marriage?

Sam's death certainly does not legitimize Joe and Sue's adultery nor nullify their need for repentance. They entered their relationship in sin, and that sin calls for confession and repentance. Sam's death does free Sue, however, from her former marital ties. ". . . but if her husband be dead, she is free from that law; so that she is no adulteress, though she be married to another man" (Romans 7:3). A possible approach to the problem of their marriage would be for Joe and Sue to have a true marriage ceremony in which they pledge their lives to each other. This would not be necessary from a legal standpoint, of course, for in the records of the state, they are considered married. But it would place both their past relationship and their future relationship in a proper light. It would likewise honor the integrity of marriage.

Hypothetical situations innumerable could be raised, which demonstrate that hard and fast rules are not always possible. Fortunately, the church must not decide every hypothetical case in order to deal with actual problems, but unfortunately, with the erosion of marriage in our society, real situations sometimes present us with problems our hypothetical situations never included.

The point here is to acknowledge that the Bible does not lay out rules for every variation of man's sinful entanglement. Christians must be obedient to the commands of Jesus in those situations which are clear, and willing to apply His principles wisely in those situations which are complicated.

IF AN ADULTEROUS RELATIONSHIP (REMARRIAGE) IS TERMINATED, SHOULD FORMER MARRIAGES BE REUNITED?

Again, this is a difficult question, and again, the guidance of a spiritual brotherhood and Spirit-filled church leaders should be sought and honored.

Some people point to the Old Testament and say no. Under Moses, a man who divorced his wife could not later take her again as his wife. "Her former husband, which sent her away, may not take her again to be his wife, after that she is defiled; for that is abomination before the LORD" (Deuteronomy 24:4).

We should observe, however, that this prohibition was given at a time when divorce was recognized, and it protected a wife from being traded back and forth according to the whim of her husband. If the New Testament sweeps away divorce itself, is it proper to go back and claim that one of the regulations for divorce still applies today?

Furthermore, to prohibit the restoration of a marriage runs us again into a logical difficulty with

Jesus' definition of marriage. How can we declare unlawful that which Jesus says is binding for life? If marital obligations, in other words, cannot be unshouldered by divorce, if in God's eyes they still stand, making remarriage adulterous, how can we forbid that a person return to his true marital obligations? Can we point to the validity of former marriage vows as reason to discontinue an adulterous relationship and then turn around and say those vows are not to be fulfilled by returning to the legitimate partner? God Himself demonstrated the righteousness of returning to one's legitimate companion, even in the context of the Old Testament prohibition. "They say, If a man put away his wife, and she go from him, and become another man's, shall he return unto her again? shall not that land be greatly polluted? but thou hast played the harlot with many lovers; yet return again to me, saith the LORD" (Jeremiah 3:1).

Oftentimes, of course, it is not possible to reunite a former marriage, and there may be times when it would be inadvisable, even if it were possible. Suppose, for example, a man married and divorced a woman and then remarried another woman. His wife turns to the Lord and remains single. The man and second woman live as husband and wife for years, and are in the process of raising a family when they too become converted. They all attend the same church. The man and second woman, in recognition of their adultery, discontinue their relationship. Would it be wise, in consideration of the children and the community, to reestablish the former relationship?

The Apostle Paul did write that according to the teaching of Jesus, reconciliation should be the objective of a separated companion. "But and if she depart, let her remain unmarried, or be reconciled to her husband" (I Corinthians 7:11). This passage, without addressing all the possible tangles which may occur in violation of marriage, holds up the objective of reconciliation where possible.

WHAT ARE SOME PRACTICAL POINTERS FOR COMMITTING ONESELF TO OBEY GOD IN SEVERING ADULTEROUS RELATIONSHIPS?

1. Distinguish between those things which can be changed and those which cannot.

The oft-quoted prayer, "Grant me the serenity to accept the things I cannot change, courage to change the things I can, and wisdom to know the difference," is fitting for those who are willing to commit themselves to obedience in leaving adulterous relationships.

Unchangeables include things for which other people are responsible—their decisions, their attitudes, their responses. These things may change, but they are beyond one's personal control.

79

Unchangeables also include the realities of the situation. For example, suppose a man has one child born to his first wife and three to a woman with whom he has been living in adultery. If that is the case, that is a reality he cannot change. Other unchangeables include present and future consequences of past sins. Pain, for example, is inevitable; though righteous responses certainly deliver a person from some pain, one cannot escape all pain. Difficult decisions, responsibilities, and obligations for such things as child care, child support, and bills (sometimes for two households) are things one cannot escape.

Unchangeables must be accepted. The more quickly we see them as such, the less we will hurt ourselves by resenting them, the less energy we will expend fighting them, and the more wisely we will be able to use our resources to cope with them.

For the Christian, accepting unchangeables is an act of faith. It is believing that God in His sovereignty is able to take these things and use them to eternal advantage.

"And we know that ALL THINGS work together for good to them that love God, to them who are the called according to his purpose. For whom he did foreknow, he also did predestinate to be conformed to the image of his Son" (Romans 8:28, 29).

Understanding that God works "all things"

together for our good certainly does not mean that we can attribute our misbehavior or its consequences to His will. This verse does indicate, however, that our devotion to God releases His powerful working in our behalf in all things.

Changeable things include our personal attitudes and responses, our habits and mannerisms, some aspects of our appearance, and our character. Many times in extended conflict with others (such as in marital difficulties), we develop habits and characteristic responses which are carnal rather than of the Spirit.

God wants us to turn our heart and mind and whole person over to His control and direction. In His hands, we can become gems of heaven, glistening with the radiance and splendor of God's own glory.

> "But we all, with open face beholding as in a glass the glory of the Lord, are changed into the same image from glory to glory, even as by the Spirit of the Lord" (II Corinthians 3:18).

2. Keep a journal of fellowship with God.

Following God through the trauma of relationship difficulties can be an emotional roller coaster. If our commitments are based on how we feel, we will make them and break them daily . . . sometimes hourly. Putting our thoughts in writing can help in several ways. First, it helps us to concentrate. Second, it helps us to verbalize and thus understand our inner feelings. And third, it helps to keep us on a steady keel. We can review. We can see where we came from. And we can better project where we want to go.

For those who commit themselves to leaving an adulterous relationship, and especially where that leaving is emotionally difficult, it is helpful to write out a commitment. For example:

> I am resolved to follow the Lord's directions for marriage. I refuse to violate His principles to satisfy my desires, believing He will stand by me and support my obedience. Furthermore, I refuse to follow any counsel which is against the righteous standards of God, whether from friends or professionals. I will from now on keep my friendships and relationships pure and carry out my responsibilities faithfully to the best of my ability.

Keeping a journal following this sort of commitment is invaluable. The journal could include struggles, prayers, insights from God's Word, promises from God's Word, helpful advice from God's people, and goals both short term and long term. The advantage of a record of one's inner life is not only that it marks the milestones of progress, but it also preserves the lessons of faith. Many of our struggles are recurring. As we face them anew, we can look back on the way God helped us through the last time. This is especially helpful where the emotional trauma is intense enough that we become forgetful.

3. Make a list of God's promises to those who obey Him.
For example:

"For the eyes of the LORD run to and fro throughout the whole earth, to shew himself strong in the behalf of them whose heart is perfect toward him" (II Chronicles 16:9).

"Not every one that saith unto me, Lord, Lord, shall enter into the kingdom of heaven; but he that doeth the will of my Father which is in heaven" (Matthew 7:21).

"And he said unto me, My grace is sufficient for thee: for my strength is made perfect in weakness" (II Corinthians 12:9).

"And the world passeth away, and the lust thereof: but he that doeth the will of God abideth for ever" (I John 2:17).

"But to this man will I look, even to him that is poor and of a contrite spirit, and trembleth at my word" (Isaiah 66:2).

These promises are from God. They assure us that those who choose to obey God have all the goodwill and grace of heaven surrounding them, upholding them, and carrying them through the difficulties of this life to eternity with God.

   4. *Choose someone with whom you can be totally honest about your struggles and make yourself accountable.*

Anyone who is willing to disentangle himself from a relationship will face inner struggles. We ought not to deny our feelings. Having someone in whom we can confide, someone who will listen with understanding, who will let us talk and then kindly help us to put things in proper perspective, who will pray with us to know and do God's will is an invaluable help in working through these difficulties.

There certainly are guidelines for keeping such a relationship healthy. We need to avoid simply digging up the past. We need to avoid repeated rehashing of other people's faults. And we must be considerate of the time and commitments of our friends—avoid monopolizing their time for our problems. But true friendship is very important in times of difficulty.

   "A friend loveth at all times, and a brother is born for adversity" (Proverbs 17:17).

   "Open rebuke is better than secret love. Faithful are the wounds of a friend. . . . Iron sharpeneth iron; so a man sharpeneth the countenance of his friend" (Proverbs 27:5, 6, 17).

HOW CAN THE CHURCH HELP?

1. The church can help by holding clearly to the Biblical standard of righteousness in an attitude of love.

This is not easy. The church at Corinth faced the problem of a man who had an immoral relationship and wished to be part of the church. He had married his stepmother. (Some believe he had not married her but was having sexual relations with her.) The Apostle Paul wrote the following in response:

> "It is reported commonly that there is fornication among you, and such fornication as is not so much as named among the Gentiles, that one should have his father's wife. . . . In the name of our Lord Jesus Christ, when ye are gathered together, and my spirit, with the power of our Lord Jesus Christ, to deliver such an one unto Satan for the destruction of the flesh, that the spirit may be saved in the day of the Lord Jesus. . . . Therefore put away from among yourselves that wicked person" (I Corinthians 5:1, 4, 5, 13).

Although excommunication is not an easy work, it is a necessary work toward those who sin by joining themselves in relationships God has forbidden.

2. The church can help those who wish to repent of adultery by being forgiving and supportive.

"Sufficient to such a man is this punishment, which was inflicted of many. So that contrariwise ye ought rather to forgive him, and comfort him, lest perhaps such a one should be swallowed up with overmuch sorrow. Wherefore I beseech you that ye would confirm your love toward him" (II Corinthians 2:6-8).

This instruction in Paul's second letter to Corinth is apparently in regard to the same man as Paul formerly had instructed the church to excommunicate. It is evidence of the value of church discipline. The man had repented. He had left his sinful relationship. And now Paul instructs the church to forgive, support, and confirm their love toward him.

When a person repents of former sin and desires to do what is right is no time for holding grudges and giving the cold shoulder, no matter how loathsome the former sin. Genuine repentance calls for genuine forgiveness and restoration.

3. The church can help people resolve tangled marriage relationships by avoiding carnal speculation and rumor.

"Thou shalt not go up and down as a talebearer among thy people" (Leviticus 19:16).

"Judge not, that ye be not judged. For with what judgment ye judge, ye shall be judged: and with what measure ye mete, it shall be measured to you again" (Matthew 7:1, 2).

"For he that will love life, and see good days, let him refrain his tongue from evil, and his lips that they speak no guile" (I Peter 3:10).

The fallen mind has a fascination with evil reports. It also has a tendency to assume evil and to put things together in the worst construction. Knowing these tendencies and the deceitfulness of the heart, Christians should avoid talk about the sins and problems of others. When they need to discuss others' failures and sins for the sake of dealing with them, they should do so with clarity and openness, but with fairness and kindness as well.

Christians need to evaluate and make conclusions and even to exercise discipline, but they are to do so with the mind of the Spirit, according to truth and love, not with suspicion, condemnation, or evil speaking.

Christians can do great damage by wagging their tongues at a time when they are dealing with those who have immoral entanglements. It is a time for seeking God, a time for prayer, a time for using discretion in what to say to whom and for what reasons.

4. The church can help those who are working out proper relationships by giving tangible help and support.

"And the multitude of them that believed were of one heart and of one soul: neither said any of them that ought of the things which he possessed was his own; but they had all things common. And with great power gave the apostles witness of the resurrection of the Lord Jesus: and great grace was upon them all. Neither was there any among them that lacked" (Acts 4:32-34).

In the context of this Scripture, many were turning to the Lord. We can assume that among the new believers there surely were those whose past lives had been immoral, though no specific list is given of the former sins of this multitude. The point is that the believers met one another's needs with the resources they had. They considered it not only an obligation, but a joy, to share thus with one another.

People who are straightening up their former immoral relationships have needs. They may need housing and financial help. They may need baby-sitting help. They may need transportation. Even if their material needs are adequately taken care of, they have deeper needs which are just as real. They need people. Loneliness is invariably a problem when marital companionship is missing, and it is especially poignant for those whose past relationships have been characterized by rejection, failure, and hurts. The church can help by visiting and by inviting these people into their homes.

5. The church can help those working through tangled relationship problems by arranging for the older to teach the younger.

"But speak thou the things which become sound doctrine: That the aged men be sober, grave, temperate, sound in faith, in charity, in patience. The aged women likewise, that they be in behaviour as becometh holiness, not false accusers, not given to much wine, teachers of good things; that they may teach the young women to be sober, to love their husbands, to love their children, to be discreet, chaste, keepers at home, good, obedient to their own husbands, that the word of God be not blasphemed. Young men likewise exhort to be sober minded" (Titus 2:1-6).

Some of this elder-to-younger teaching can be informal in the normal round of visiting and hospitality. It can be, but it likely won't be unless there is instruction and encouragement for it to be so.

Beyond this, however, it is healthy for the church to arrange for appointments between the older and the younger as the need may be. Such an "appointment" may be the informal suggestion to an older Christian to spend time with a younger Christian. It may be the recommendation of the church or church leaders for an older person to counsel regularly one who needs help. It may be regular Bible studies, arranged either privately or under the direction of the church leaders. In any case, such arrangements can be of tremendous help to younger Christians in general and those working through marital entanglements in particular.

WHAT CAN THE CHURCH DO TO BUILD STRONG HOMES AND RESIST THE EROSION OF MARRIAGES IN THE CHURCH?

In addition to the suggestions given in answer to the former question, the church should lift up a high moral standard and should strongly support the family unit.

1. Church leaders should teach and be an example of a high moral standard.

"Preach the word; be instant in season, out of season; reprove, rebuke, exhort with all longsuffering and doctrine. For the time will come when they will not endure sound doctrine; but after their own lusts shall they heap to themselves teachers, having itching ears" (II Timothy 4:2, 3).

"Be thou an example of the believers . . . in

90

purity. Rebuke not an elder, but intreat him as a father; and the younger men as brethren; the elder women as mothers; the younger as sisters, with all purity" (I Timothy 4:12; 5:1, 2).

Those who are immoral want teachers and preachers and counselors who cater to their lusts, who tell them their marital sins are understandable. The pure church, however, needs ministers who will stand for the truth with clarity and love. Ministers today must live pure lives themselves, exercising discretion in the way they relate to women. What minister can effectively stem the tide of impurity at his church door who violates Jesus' teaching in his own marriage?

Ministers need to instruct their people in what the Bible says about marriage, about divorce, and about remarriage. This can be done through sermons as well as through literature. If ever a people needed to know the truth about such issues, it is the people of our day.

2. Church leaders should encourage healthy family interaction.

Many church leaders today mistakenly think that a highly organized program is necessary for the needs of families in the church. Unfortunately, there is often so much going, so many good things for toddlers, juniors, teens, and every other age group, that the family unit is actually being pulled apart.

It's time to slow down. Families need to be taught to do things as families. God instructs fathers and mothers to talk to their children "when thou sittest in thine house, and when thou walkest by the way, and when thou liest down, and when thou risest up" (Deuteronomy 6:7). For many families, "sitting in the house" and "walking by the way" are activities of a different age.

One of the major problems in today's families is that fathers, mothers, and children spend too little time together. Fathers face the pressures of being a success at work. Many mothers have entered the work force either for the personal satisfaction of a career or to increase the family income. Many homes in Western culture today are reaping the consequences of fragmentation as a direct result of both father and mother pursuing their own interests outside the home.

Parents need to be taught the priority of family life. "Every wise woman buildeth her house" (Proverbs 14:1). As much as possible, mothers should be "keepers at home" (Titus 2:5). Husbands "ought to love their wives [not their jobs] as their own bodies," and commit themselves to rearing their children "in the nurture and admonition of the Lord" (Ephesians 5:28; 6:4).

3. Church leaders should assist parents in guarding their homes against the pressures of immorality.

"And have no fellowship with the unfruitful works of darkness, but rather reprove them. For it is a shame even to speak of those things which are done of them in secret" (Ephesians 5:11, 12).

"For what fellowship hath righteousness with unrighteousness? and what communion hath light with darkness.... Wherefore come out from among them, and be ye separate, saith the Lord, and touch not the unclean thing; and I will receive you, and will be a Father unto you, and ye shall be my sons and daughters" (II Corinthians 6:14, 17, 18).

One of the direct pipelines of sin into Western homes today is television. Through TV many parents unthinkingly invite adulterers, cheaters, liars, and murderers into the family room and allow these people to entertain the whole family with their sin for hours on end. The average amount of time family members spend per day associating with these TV characters is significantly higher than the amount of time they spend in meaningful interaction with each other. Is it any wonder our age is producing people who are unfaithful in their marriages?

The Bible says we are not to have fellowship with the wicked and that it is shameful even to speak of what they do in private. How much less ought we to find their sinfulness entertaining!

Many Christians today who are serious about building their homes for Christ do not permit television in their homes. Furthermore, they reject other forms of worldly entertainment such as movies, videos, radio programs, music, and magazines which cater to the "lust of the flesh, and the lust of the eyes, and the pride of life" (I John 2:16). If God's people wish to raise up a moral standard which keeps marriages and homes solid, they must not only teach sound morals, but also make their homes havens against the evils of the world.

CONCLUSION

We can summarize the teaching of Jesus and the apostles on our subject in three simple statements:

1. Marriage is for life.

2. Divorce of a lawful companion is wrong.

3. Remarriage while one's former partner is still living is adulterous and continues to be so as long as the relationship continues.

Today, those who wish to follow the teaching of Jesus and the apostles in these matters find themselves in the minority, even among professed Christians. If the Biblical position is to be maintained, ministers must be faithful in teaching it and living pure lives themselves. Men and women of God must joyfully accept their roles and responsibilities as God has ordained. The church and home must cooperate in maintaining strong family units. And parents must order their homes in the ways of holiness and truth, and keep their homes free from worldly influences.

May the Lord raise up fathers and mothers and sons and daughters who have the courage to live for God and leave a testimony of faith in this sinful and adulterous generation.

"When the Son of man cometh, shall he find faith on the earth?" (Luke 18:8).

ENDNOTES

1. W. W. Davies, "Divorce in O.T.," *International Standard Bible Encyclopedia* (Grand Rapids, Mich.: Wm. B. Eerdmans Publishing Co., 1956).

2. Jerome, Letter LV, *Nicene and Post-Nicene Fathers*, Vol. 6, tr. Philip Schaff, p. 110.

3. Another understanding of *porneia* which has gained some acceptance recently is that *porneia* here is a legal term. In Leviticus 18, various close-kin marriages were forbidden—a man, for example, was not permitted to marry his aunt or his sister. According to this understanding, the Pharisees had asked a legal question, "Is it LAWFUL for a man to put away his wife for any cause?" Jesus then gave an answer with a legal exception. He said, in essence, "Anyone who puts away his wife, excepting the putting away of an unlawful wife (*porneia*), and marries another is committing adultery." Support for this view rests in that the term *porneia* is used in the Septuagint to refer to these unlawful relationships in Leviticus 18. Two New Testament examples of unlawful relationships include Herod, who married his brother's wife and was told "It is not LAWFUL for thee to have thy brother's wife" (Mark 6:18); and the man at Corinth, whose sin of

having his father's wife was termed *porneia* (I Corinthians 5:1). This view, like the espousal view, is consistent with Jesus' basic position: no divorce, no remarriage. It seems a rather obvious exception, however, one that would hardly need mention either to the Jews or to modern readers. Furthermore, no early writer understood the exception clause in this way.

4. Anon., "Scars of Divorce," published by Gospel Tract Society, Inc., Independence, Mo., pp. 1, 3, 6.

5. John Coblentz, *Christian Family Living* (Harrisonburg, Va.: Christian Light Publications, Inc., 1992), pp. 167-170.

❈ ❈ ❈ ❈ ❈ ❈ ❈ ❈

Christian Light Publications, Inc., is a nonprofit conservative Mennonite publishing company providing Christ-centered, Biblicial literature in a variety of forms including Gospel tracts, books, Sunday school materials, summer Bible school materials, and a full curriculum for Christian day schools and home schools.

For more information at no obligation or for spiritual help, please write to us at:

Christian Light Publications
P. O. Box 1126
Harrisonburg, VA 22801-1126